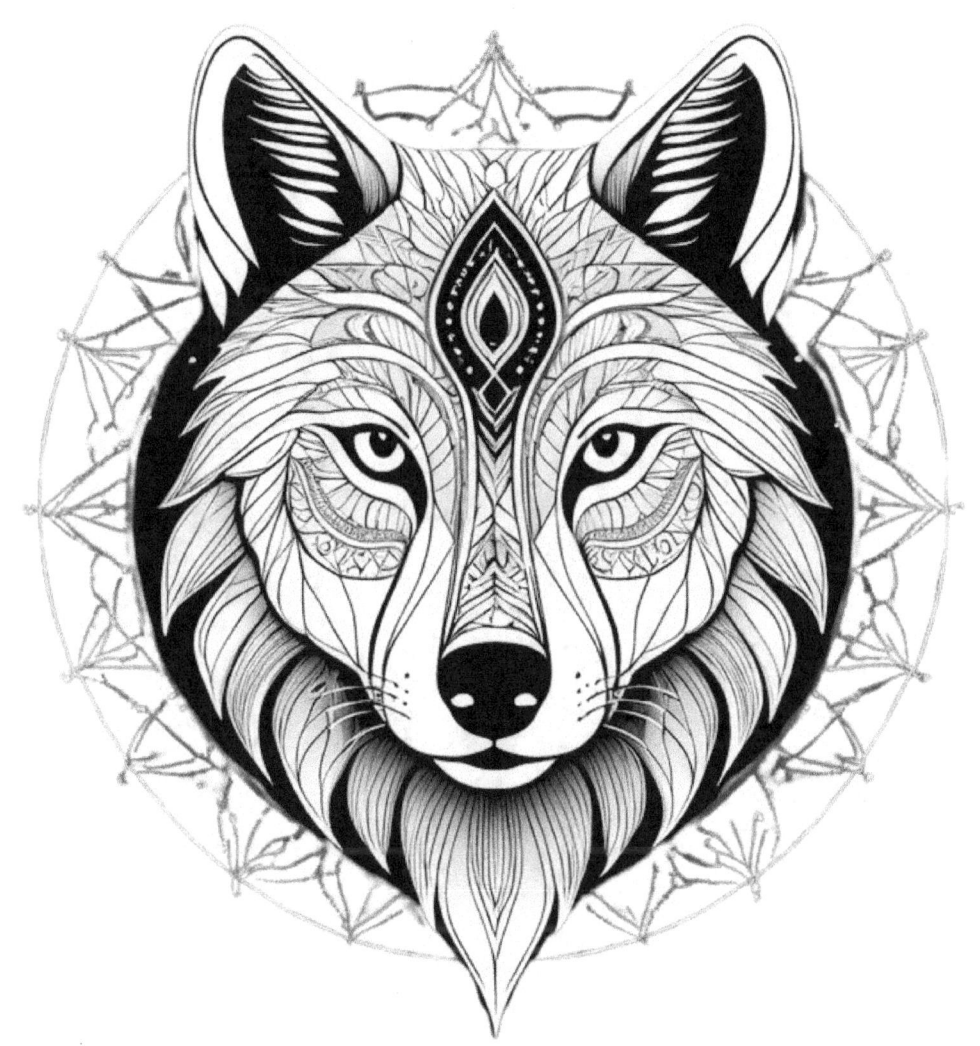

I am worthy of love and respect

1

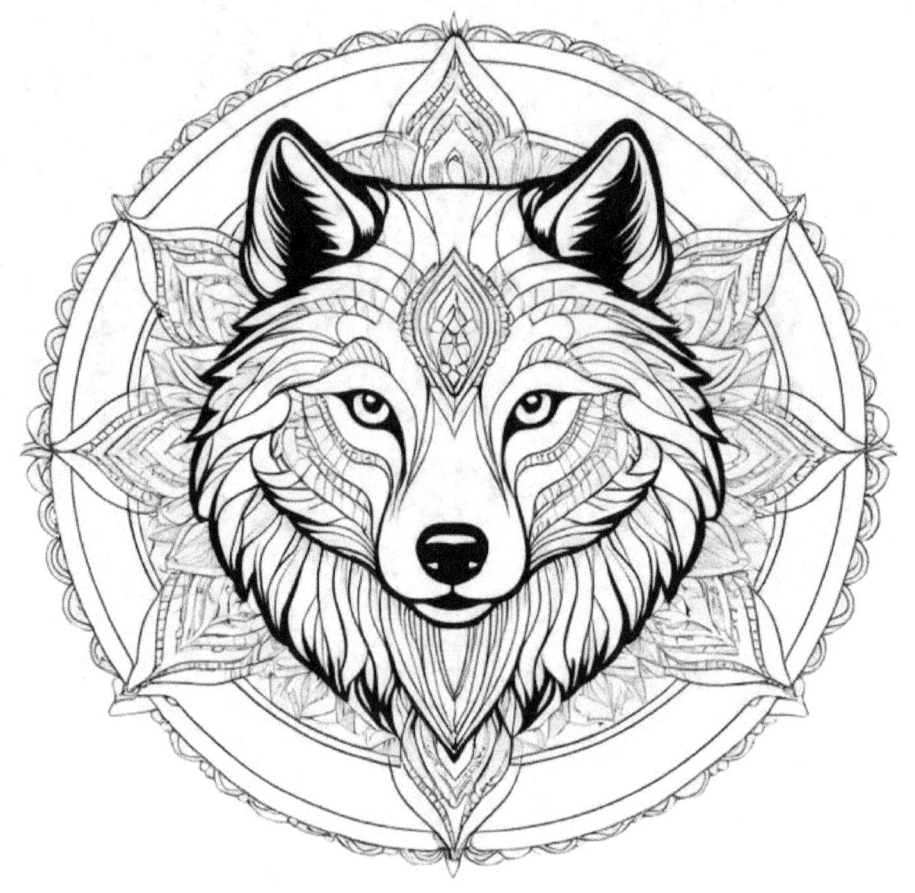

I believe in myself and my abilities

2

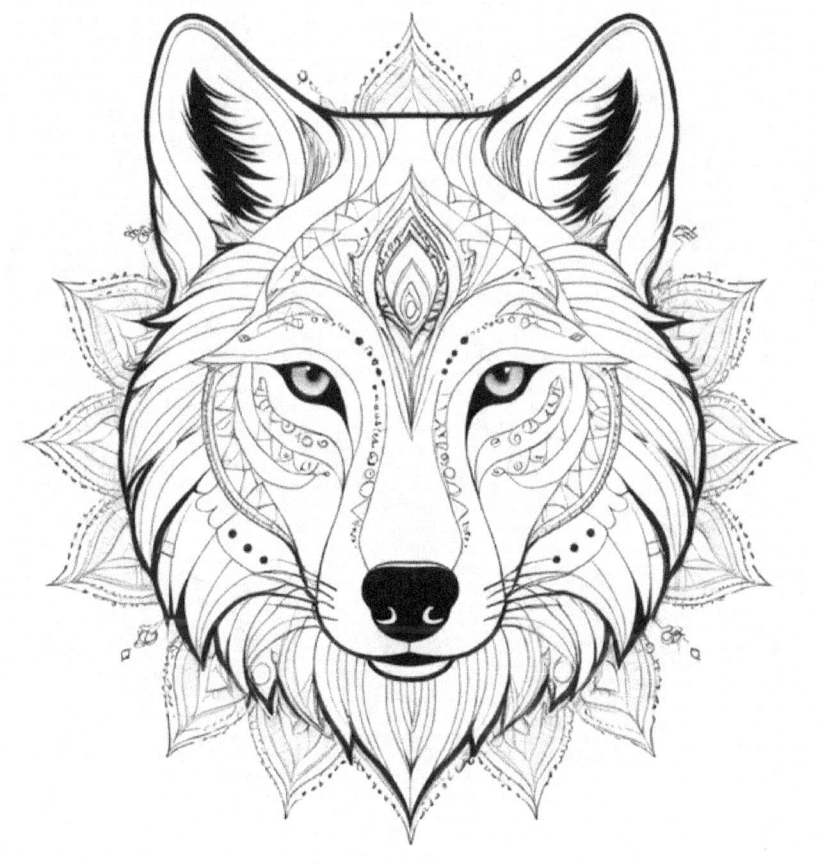

I deserve happiness and fulfillment

3

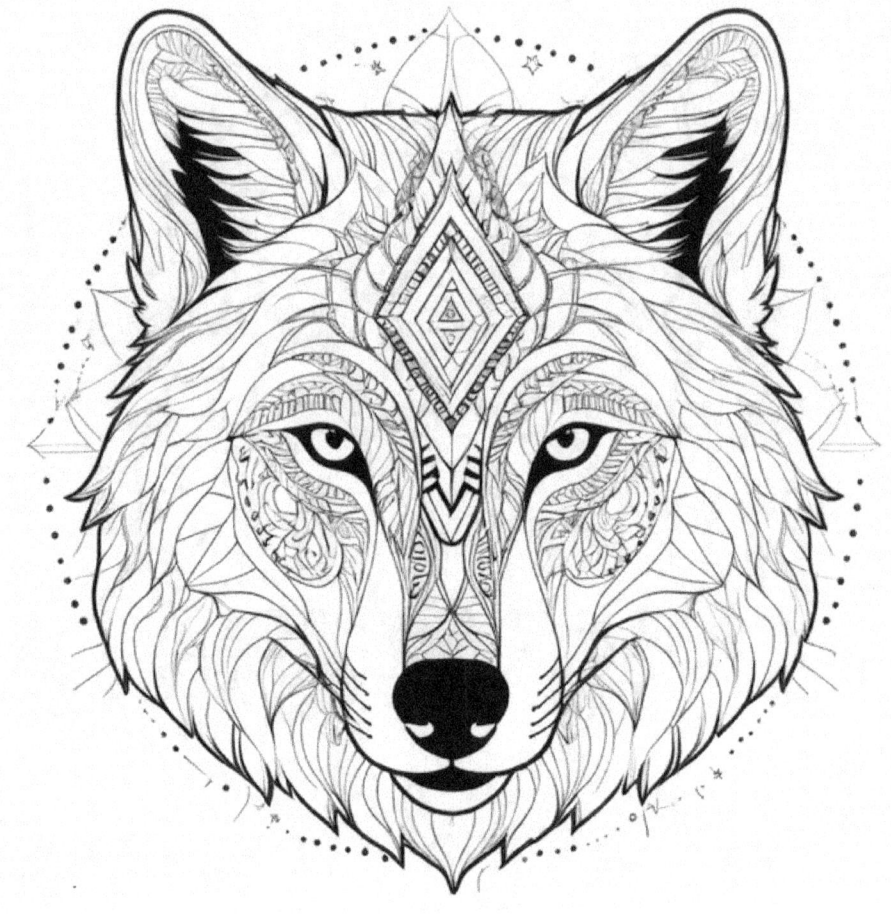

I am enough just as I am

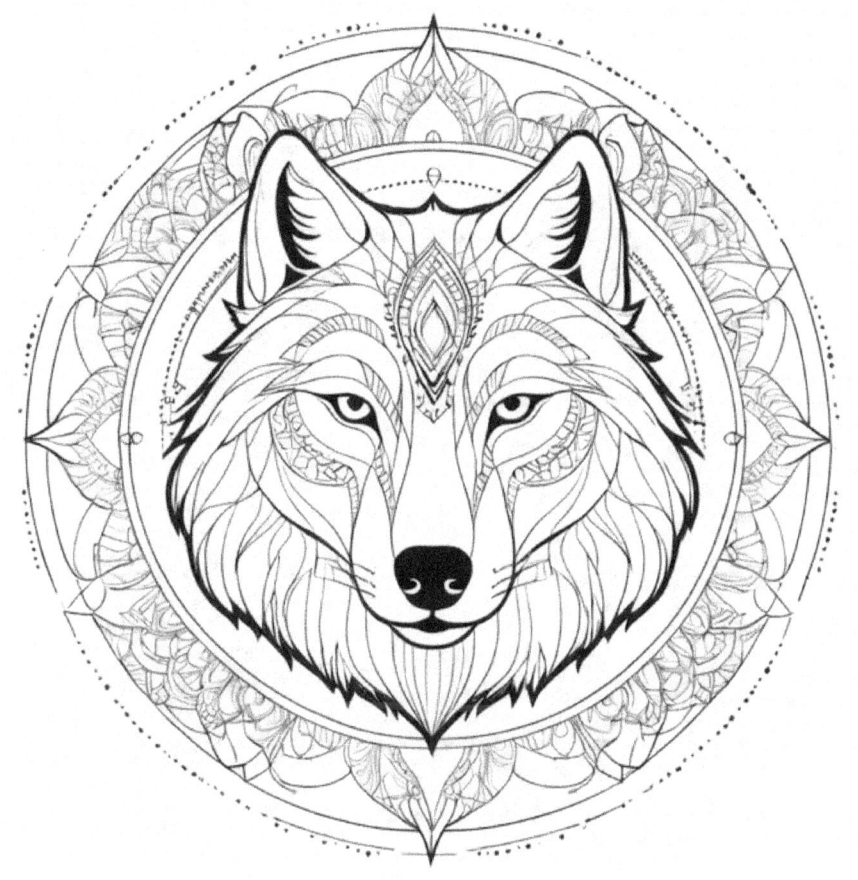

I embrace my imperfections and celebrate my uniqueness.

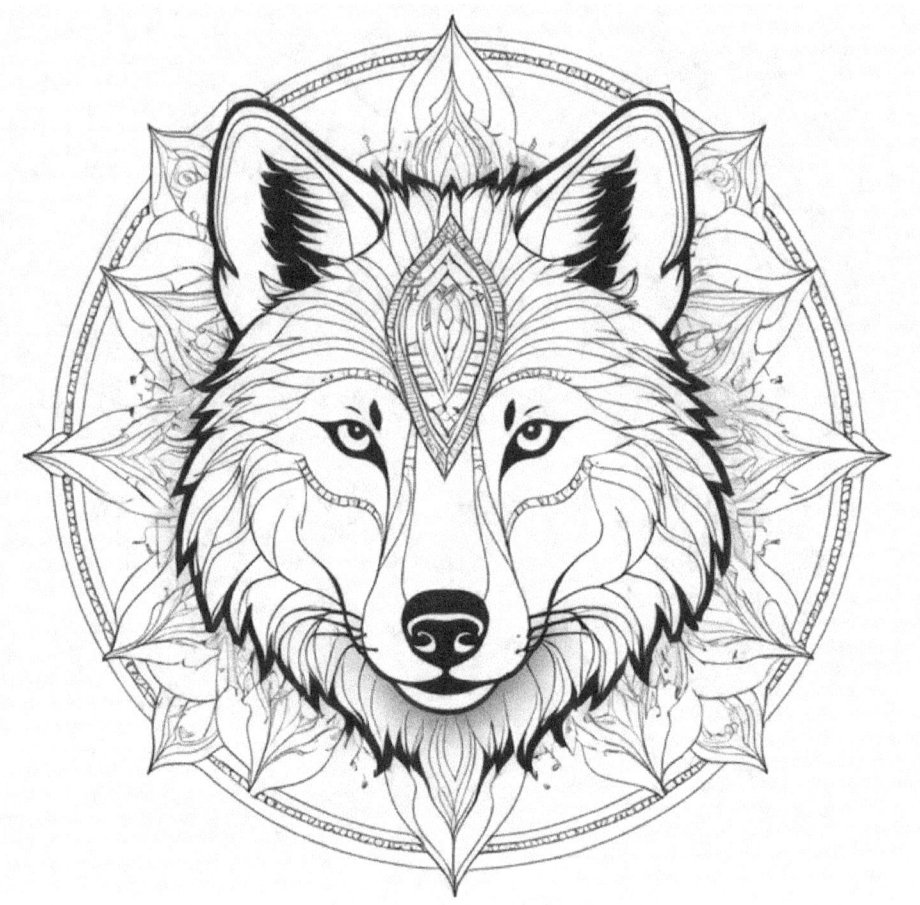

I trust in my capacity to overcome challenges.

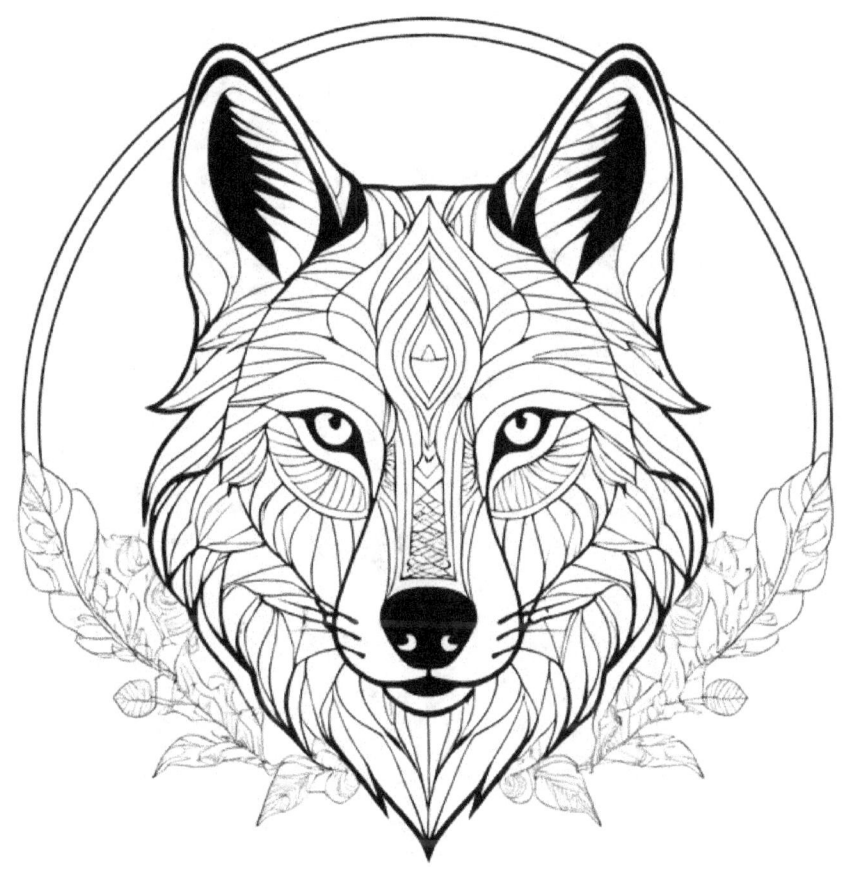

I am proud of who I am becoming.

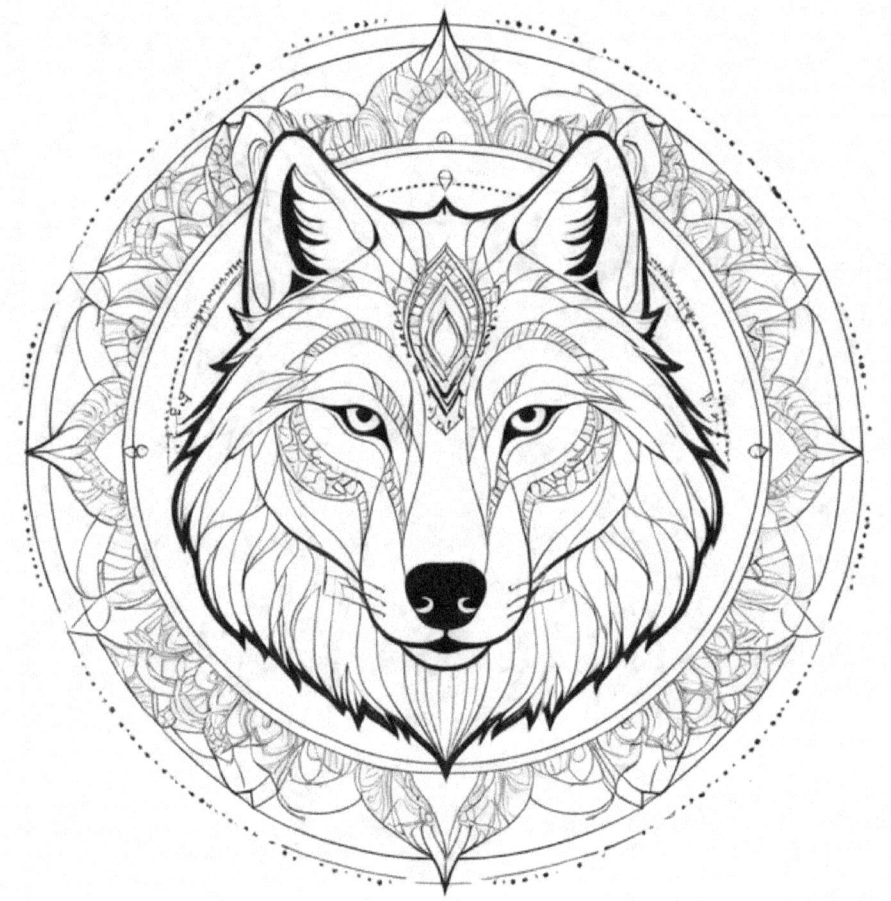

"I am deserving of success and prosperity.

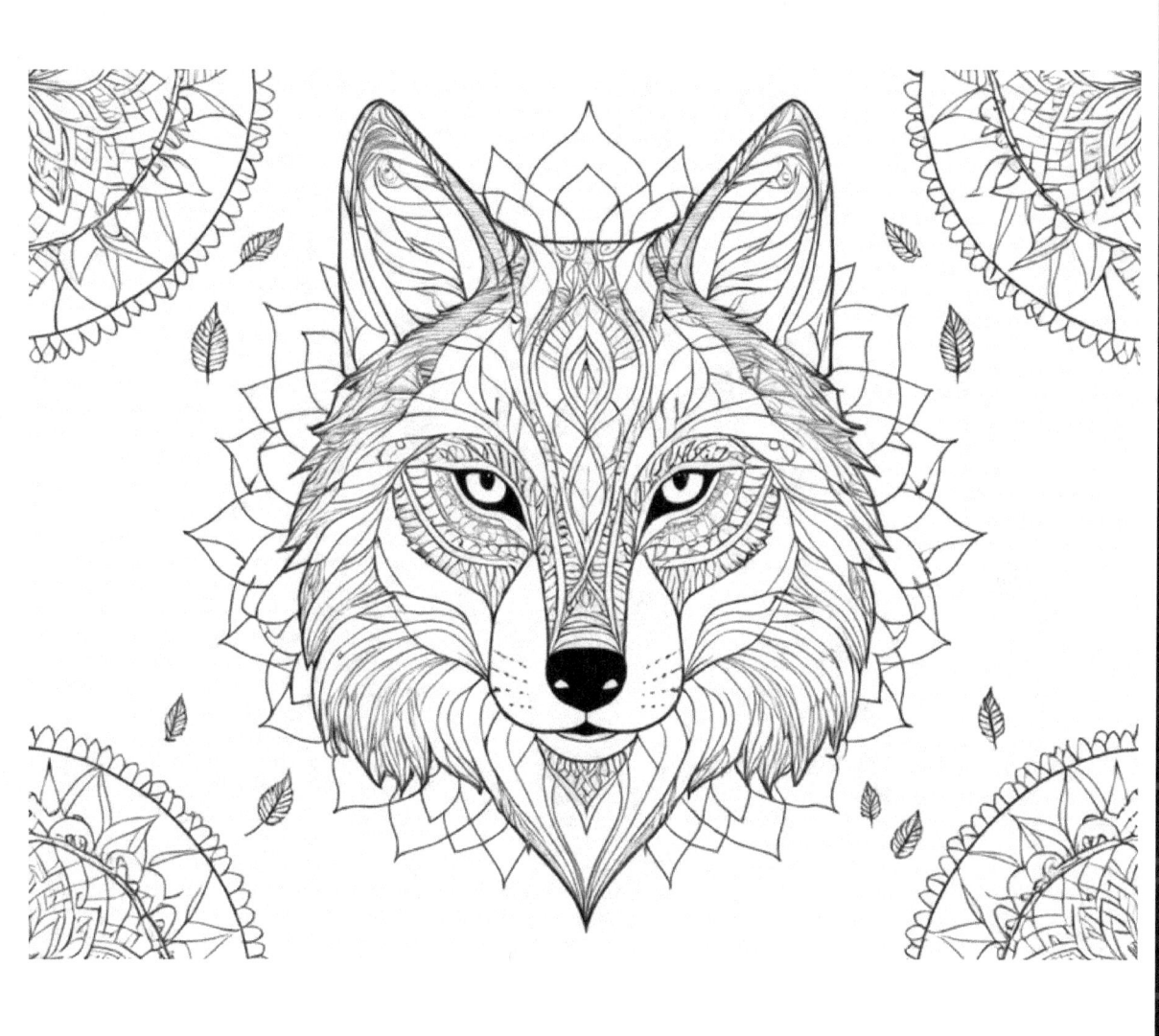

I radiate confidence and positivity

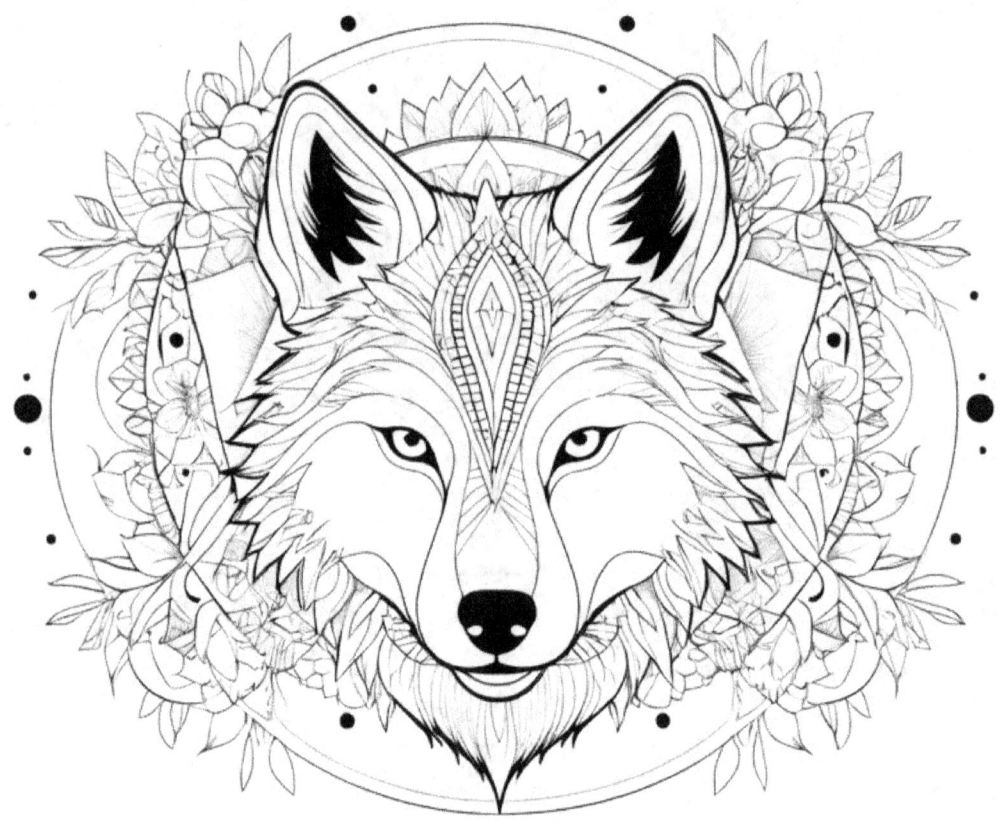

I am capable of achieving my goals.

10

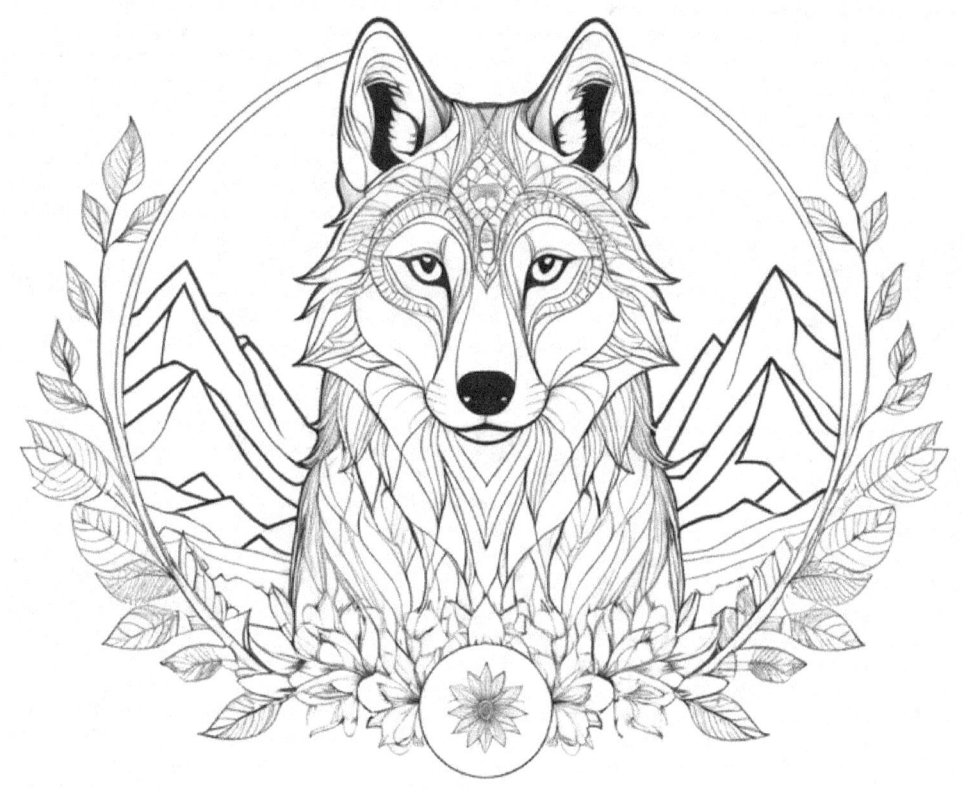

I am deserving of love and kindness

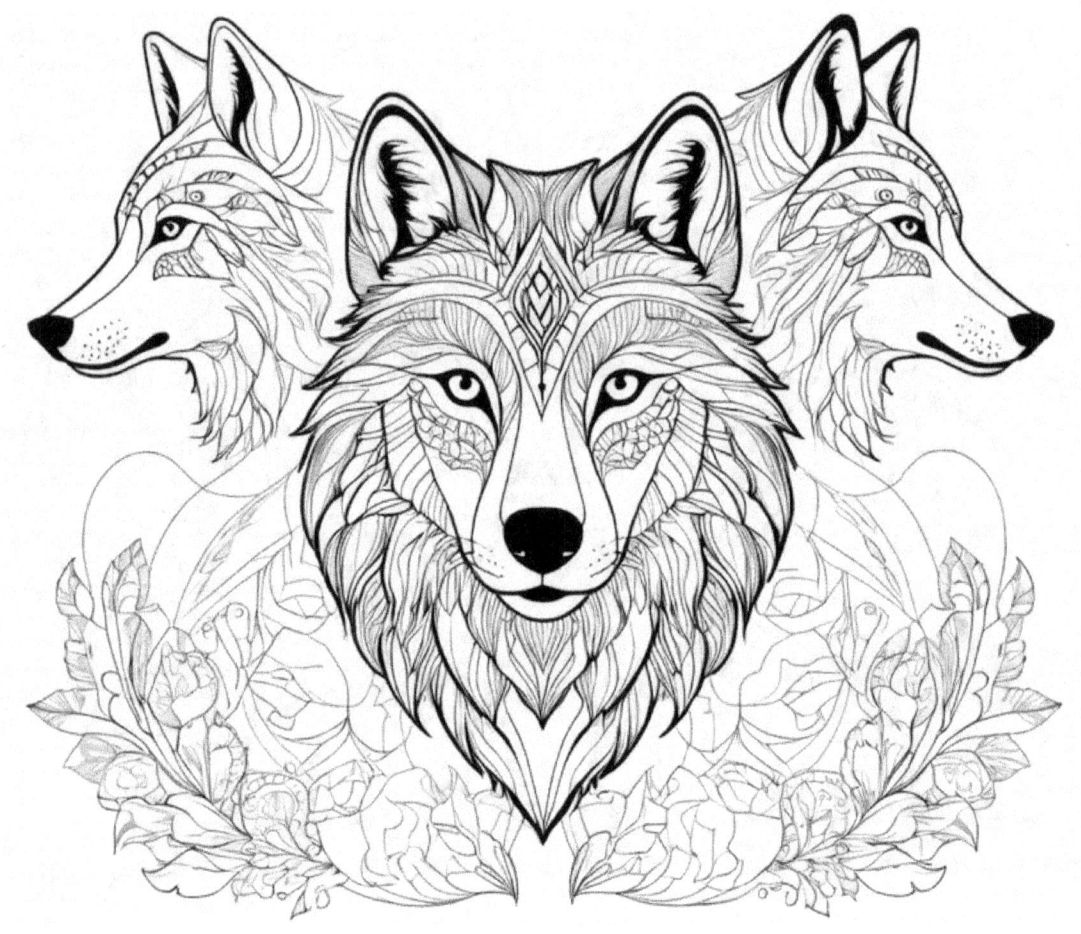

I choose to focus on the good in myself and others.

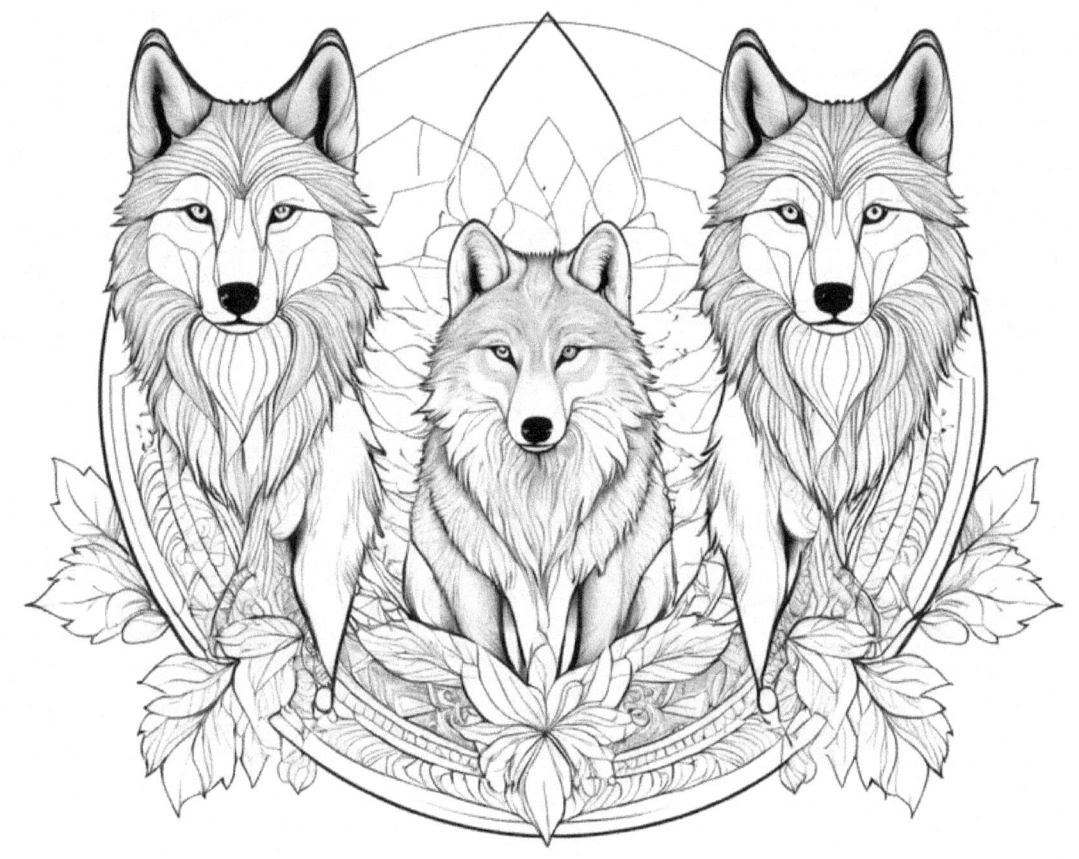

I am resilient and can bounce back from setbacks.

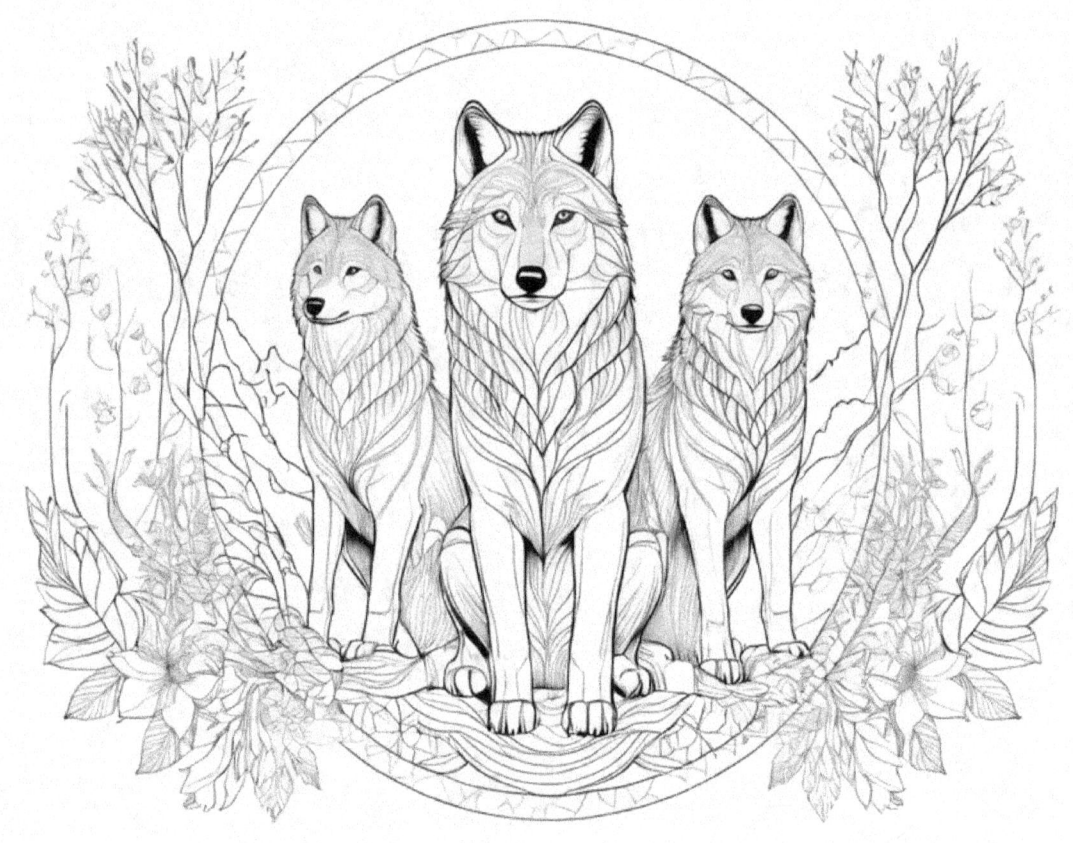

I am worthy of all the good things life has to offer.

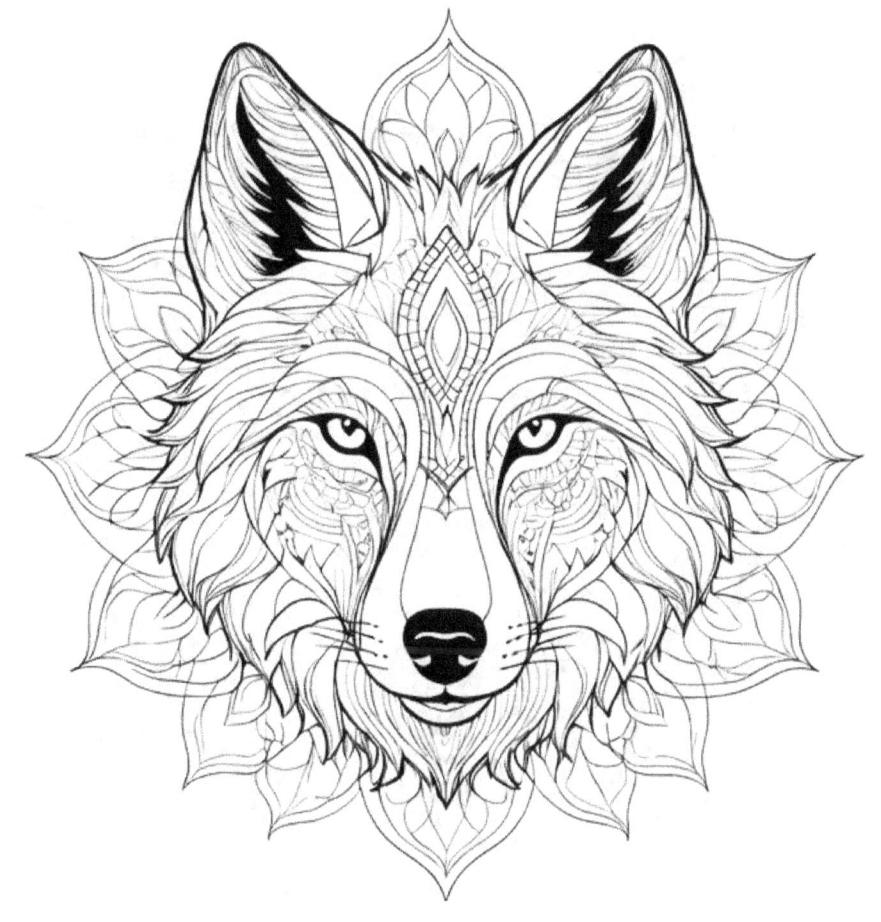

I accept myself unconditionally.

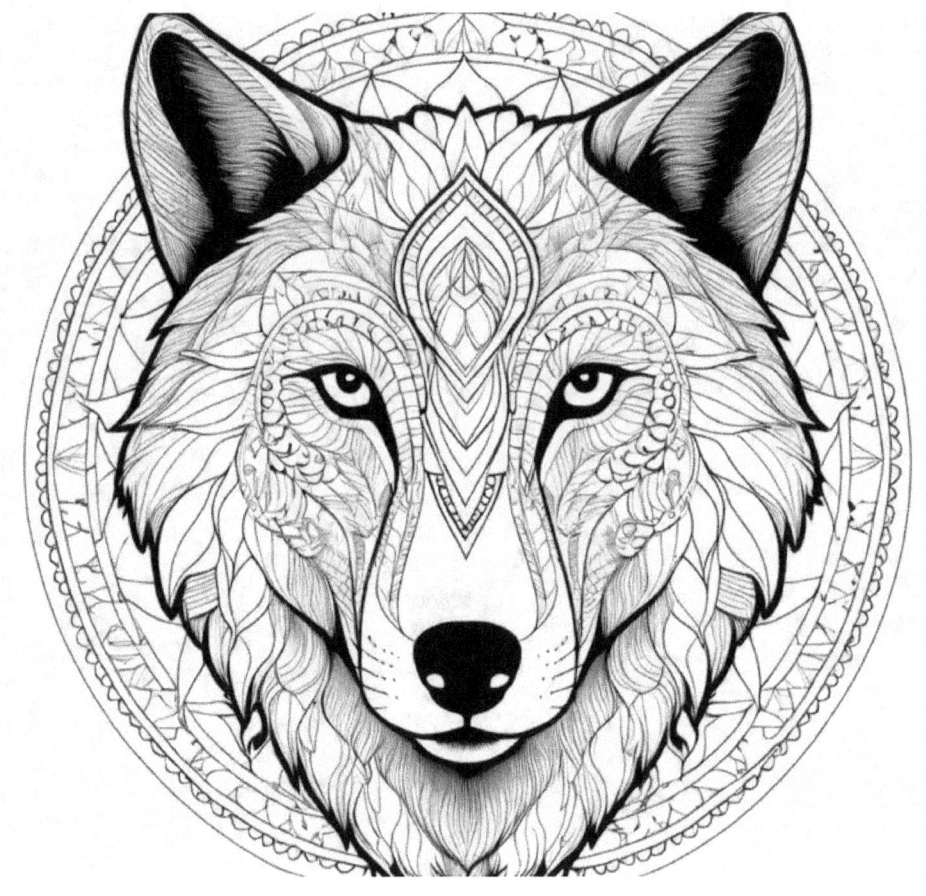

I am a work in progress, and that's okay

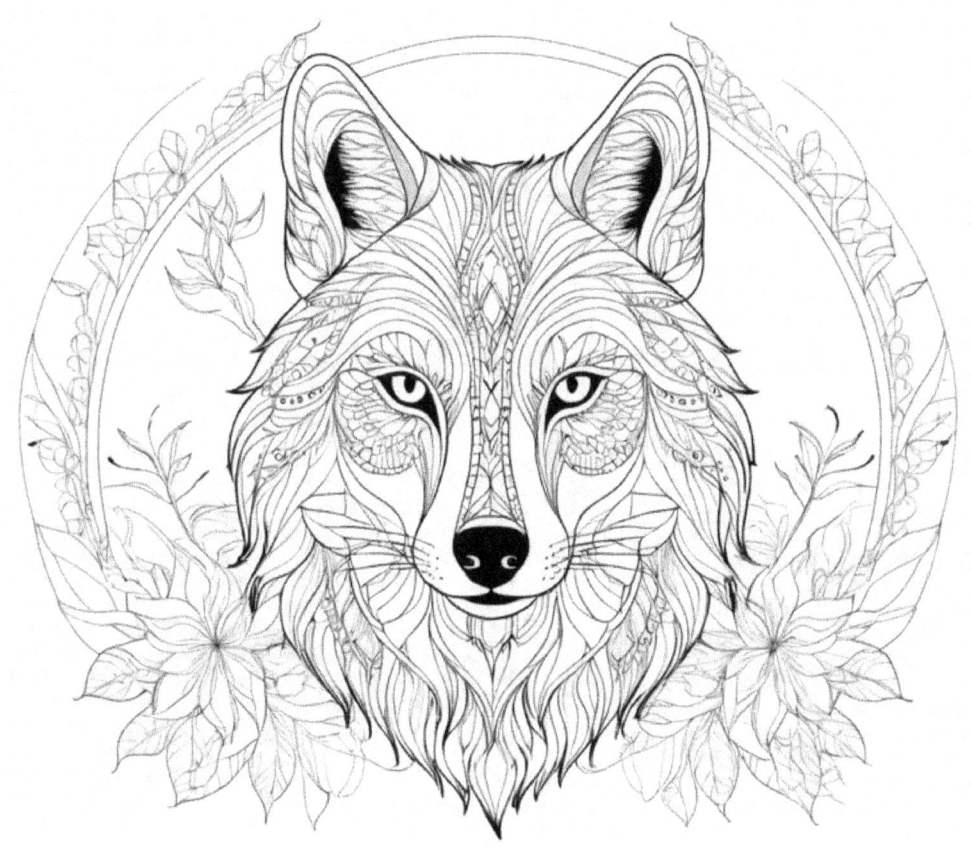

"I am strong, capable, and worthy of respect."

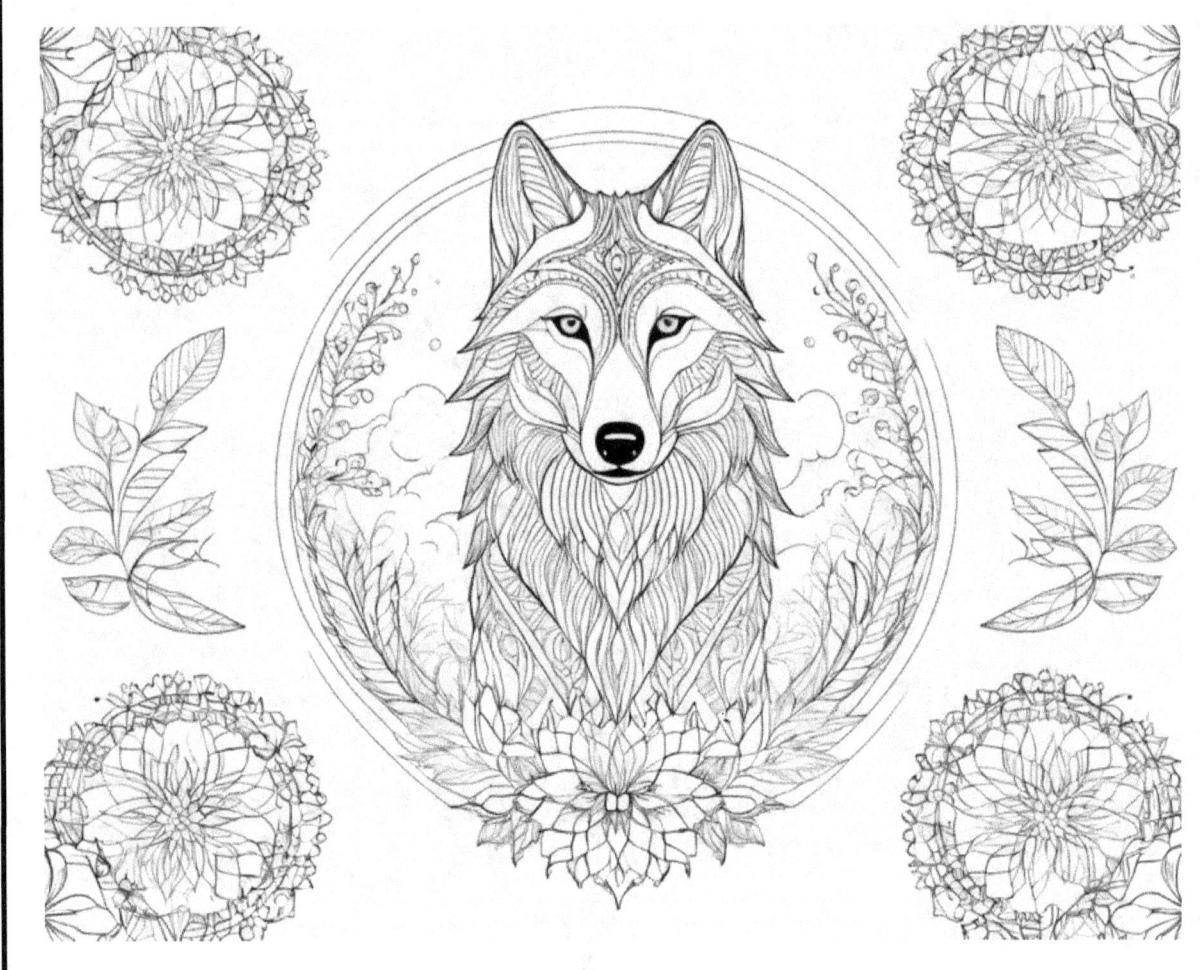

I am in control of my own happiness.

18

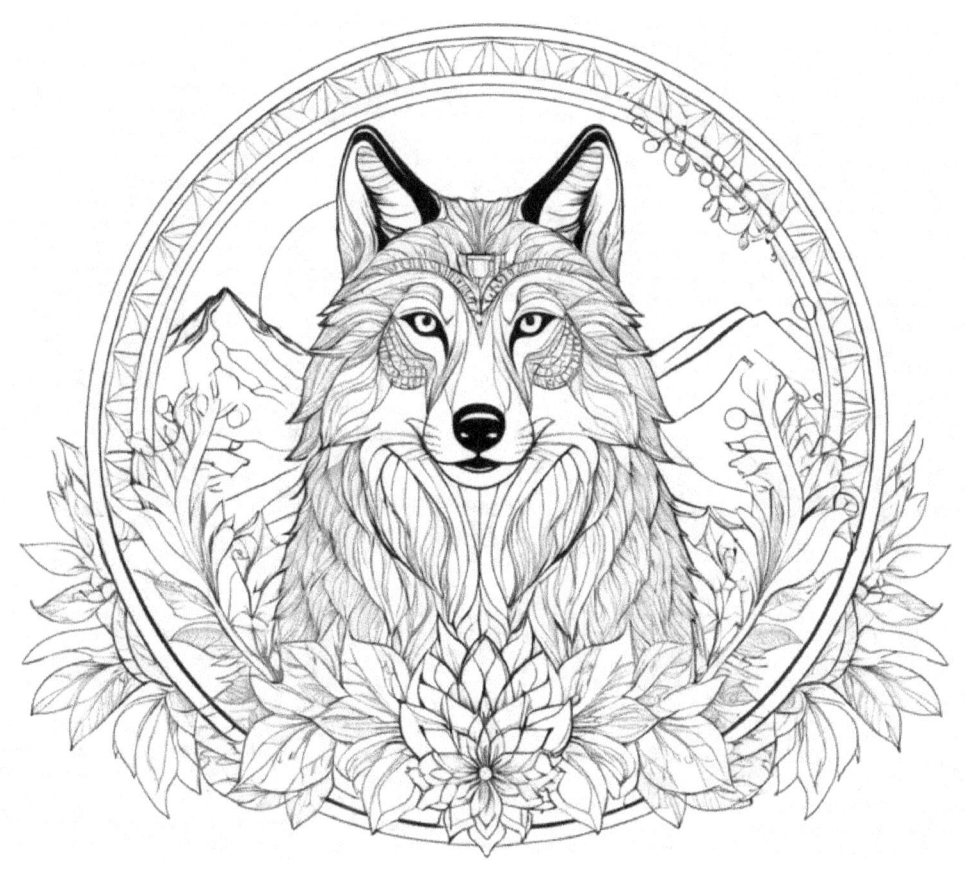

I trust in my intuition and inner wisdom

19

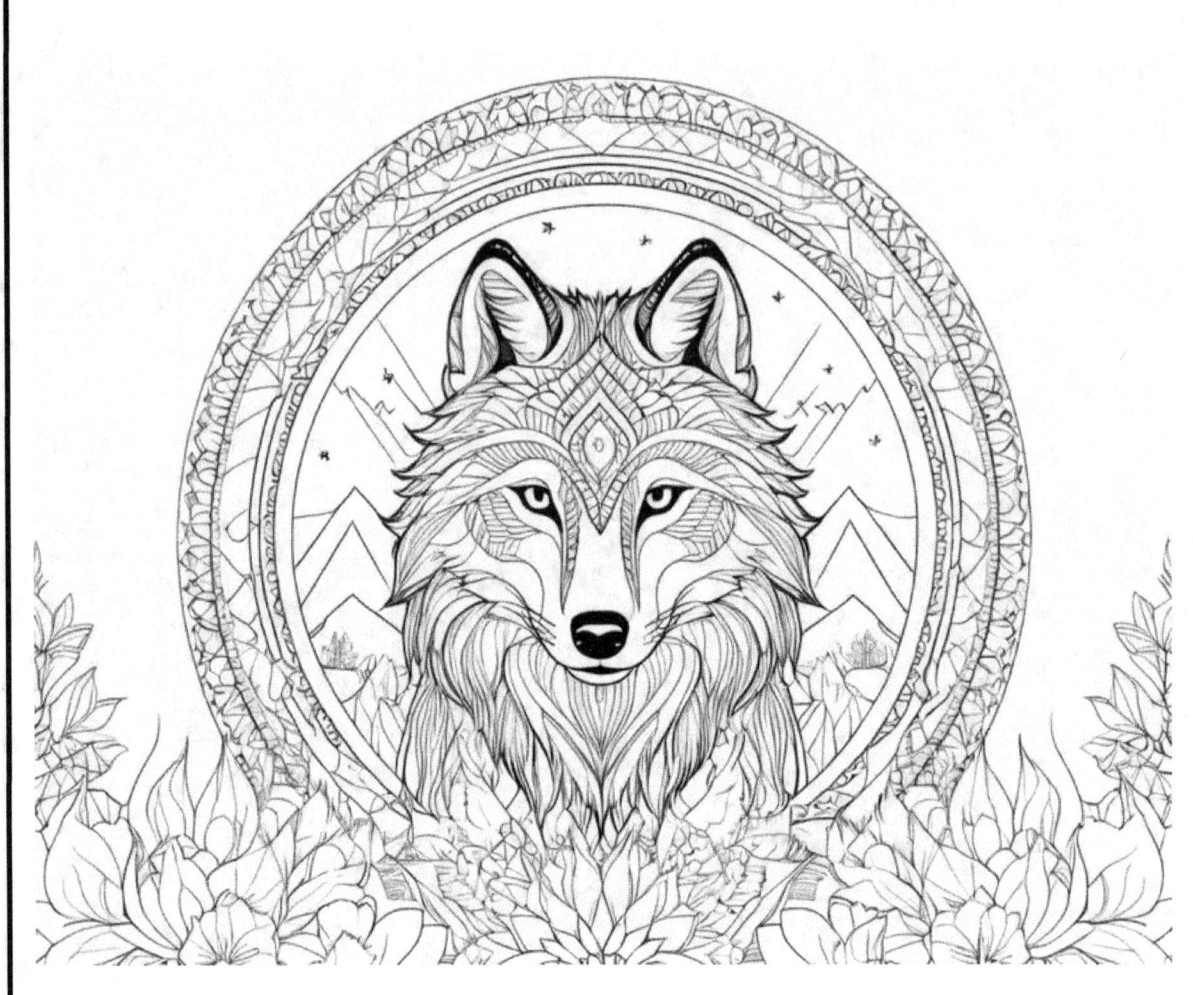

I am valuable and deserving of self-care.

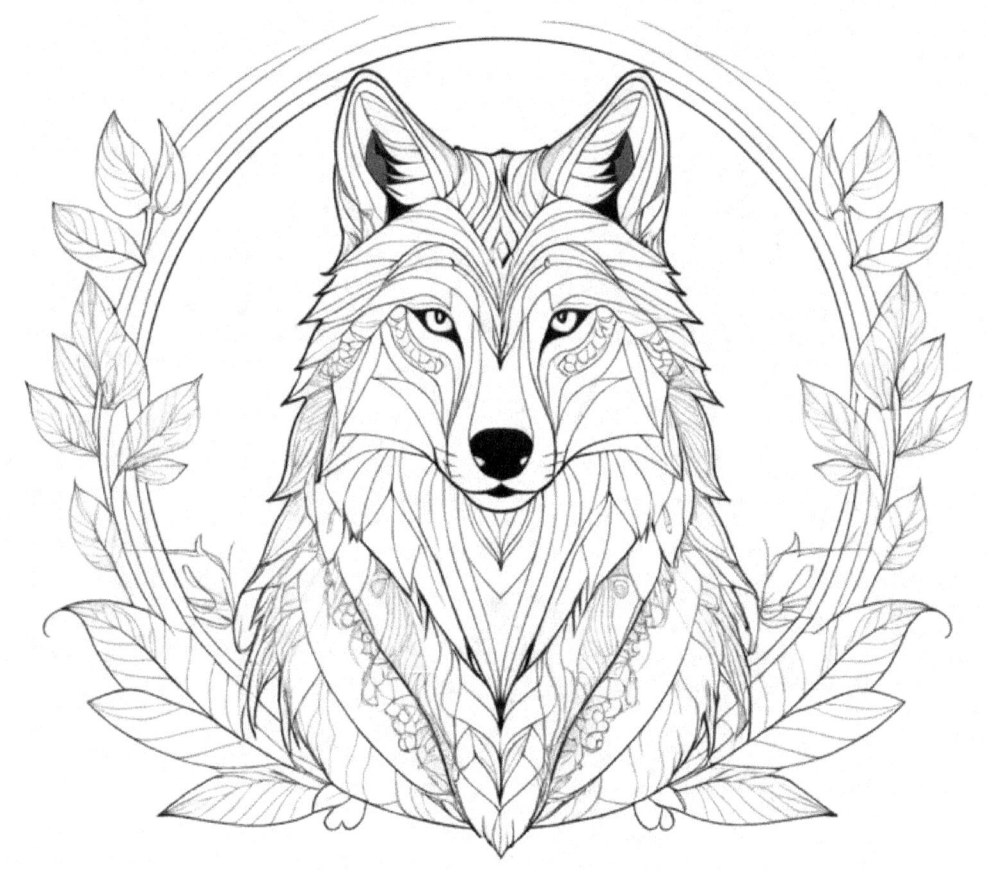

I am a unique individual with much to offer the world.

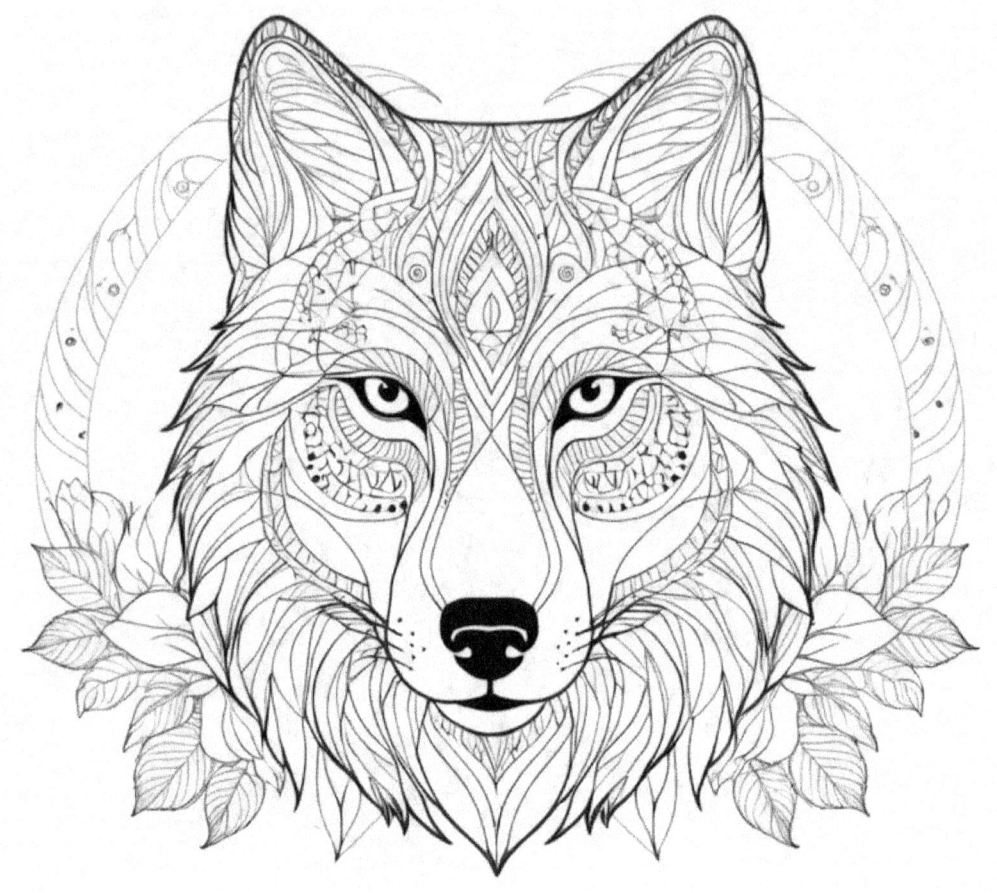

I release self-doubt and embrace self-assurance.

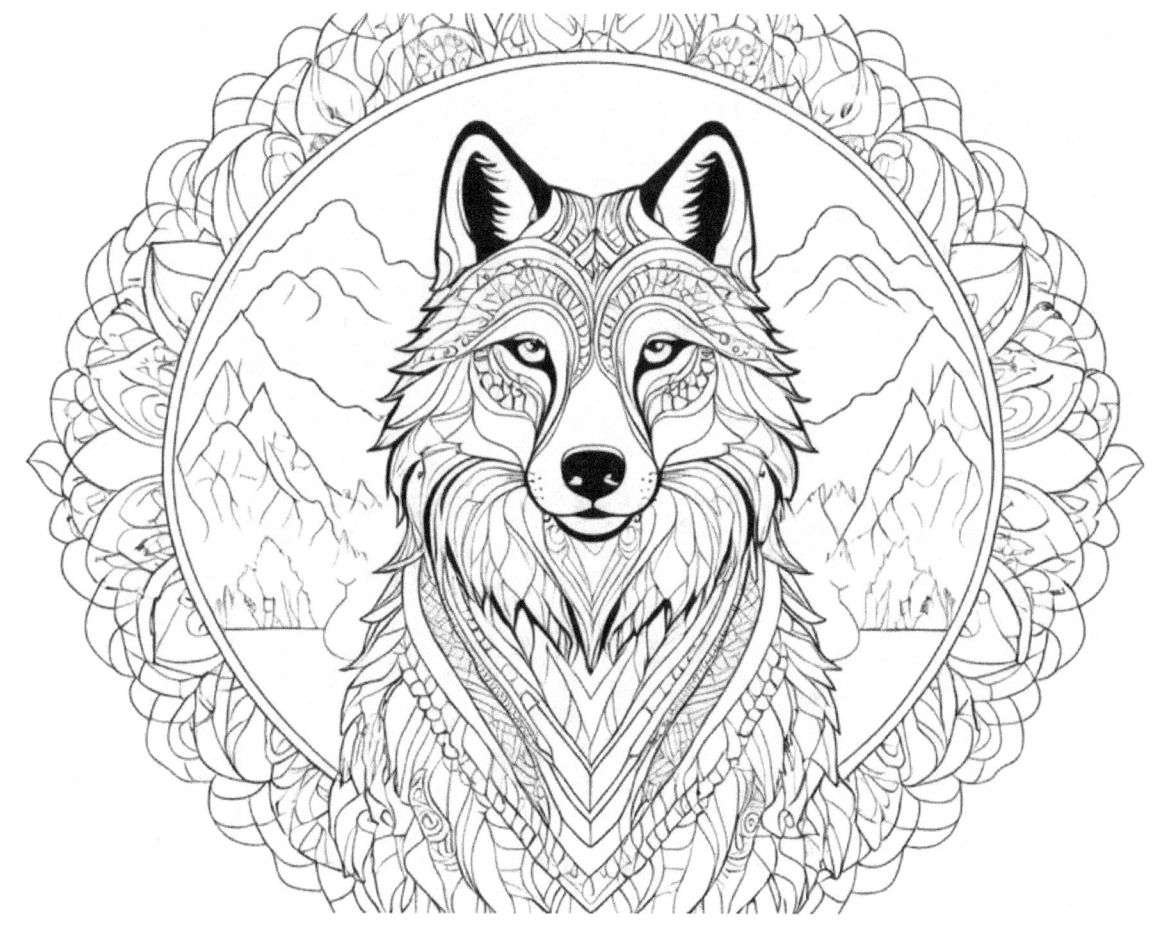

Your potential for growth is limitless.

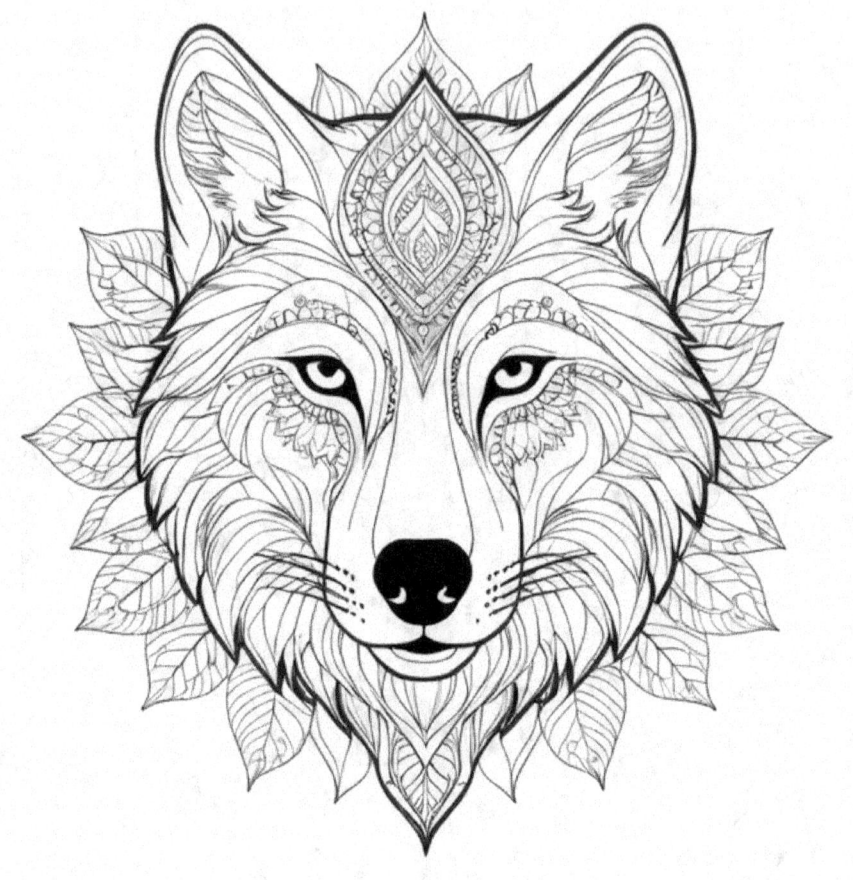

I am deserving of success and abundance

24

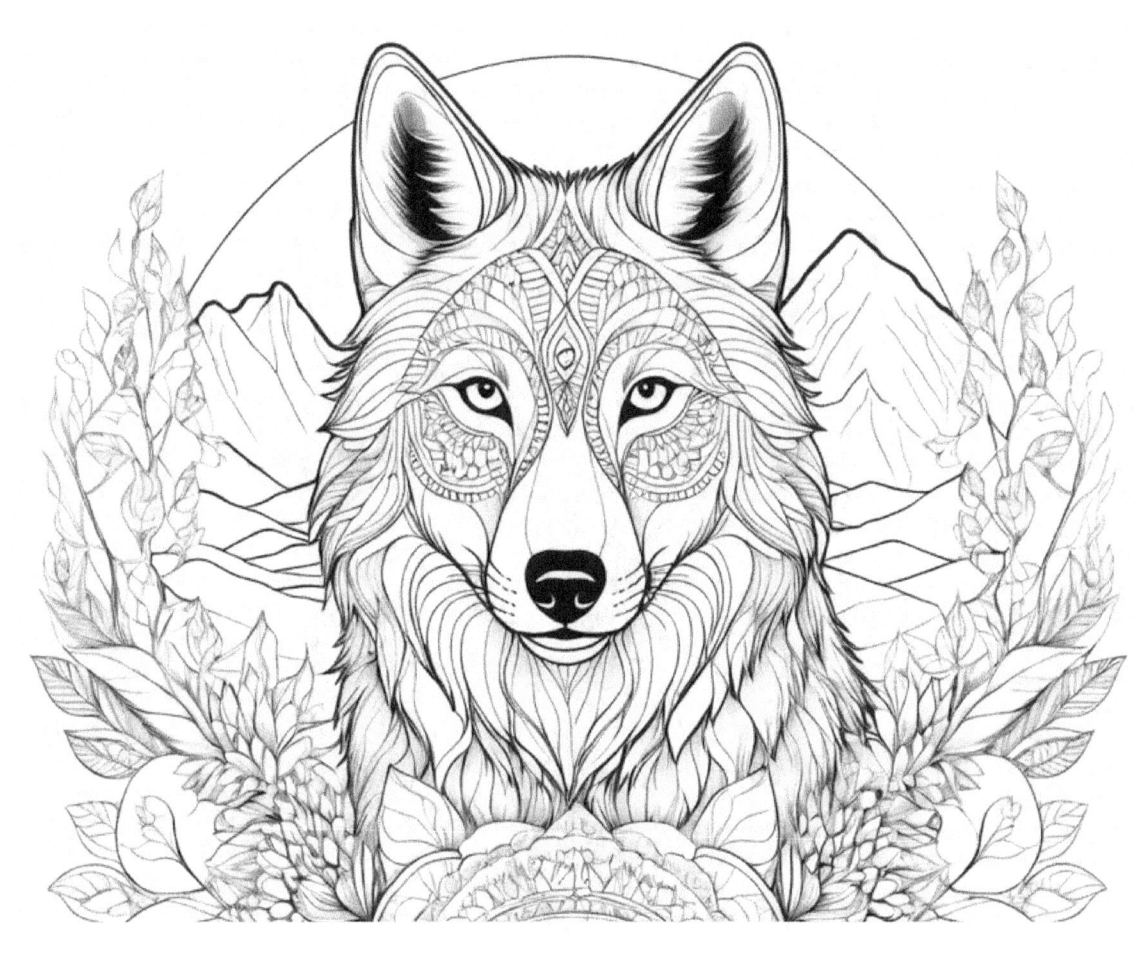

I am learning and growing every day.

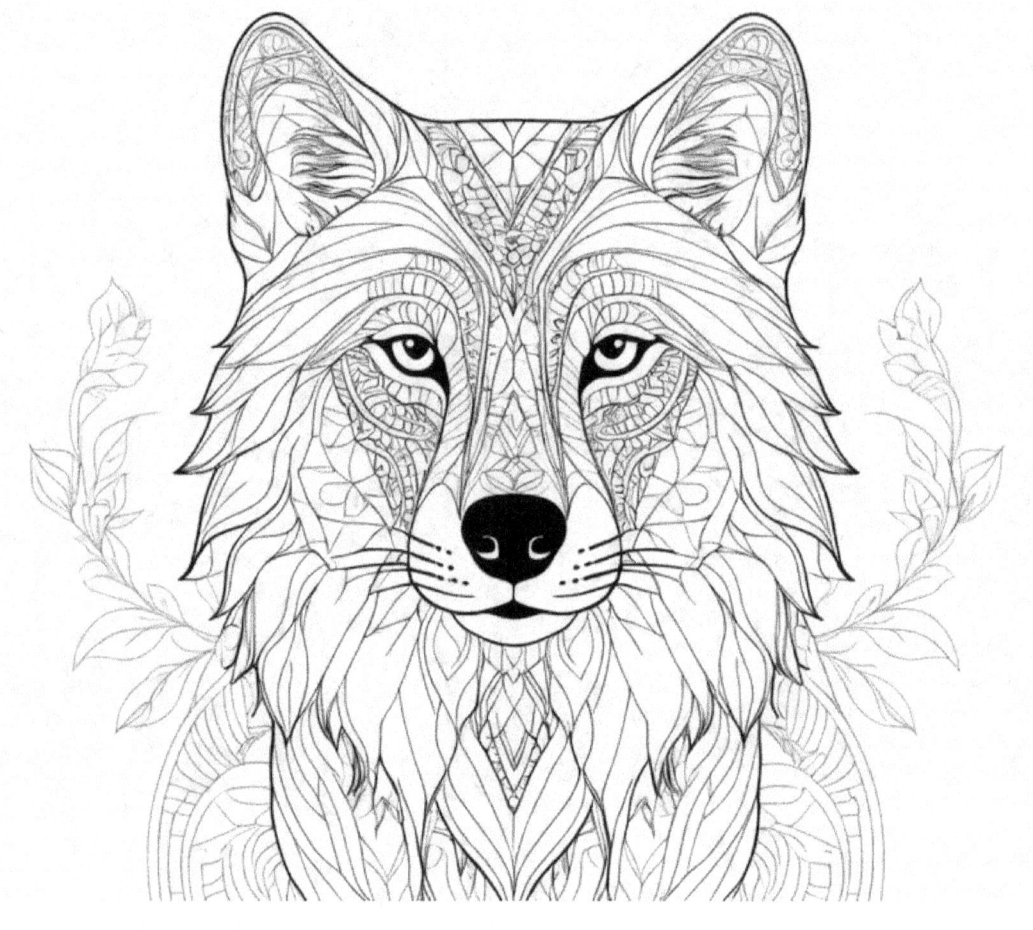

I am the architect of my own destiny